A SURVIVAL GUIDE

THE ATTACK OF THE

# ALIENS

BY
HERMIONE
REDSHAW

# BookLife
## PUBLISHING

©2023
BookLife Publishing Ltd.
King's Lynn, Norfolk
PE30 4LS, UK

All rights reserved.
Printed in Poland.

A catalogue record for this book is available from the British Library.

ISBN: 978-1-80155-886-0

**Written by:**
Hermione Redshaw

**Edited by:**
William Anthony

**Designed by:**
Drue Rintoul

# AN INTRODUCTION TO BOOKLIFE RAPID READERS...

Packed full of gripping topics and twisted tales, BookLife Rapid Readers are perfect for older children looking to propel their reading up to top speed. With three levels based on our planet's fastest animals, children will be able to find the perfect point from which to accelerate their reading journey. From the spooky to the silly, these roaring reads will turn every child at every reading level into a prolific page-turner!

## CHEETAH

The fastest animals on land, cheetahs will be taking their first strides as they race to top speed.

## MARLIN

The fastest animals under water, marlins will be blasting through their journey.

## FALCON

The fastest animals in the air, falcons will be flying at top speed as they tear through the skies.

Photo Credits – Images are courtesy of Shutterstock.com. With thanks to Getty Images, Thinkstock Photo and iStockphoto. 2–3 – Anastacia – azzzya. 4–5 – Lario Tus, Dean Drobot. 6–7 – Virrage Images, Jakub Krechowicz. 8–9 – Independent birds, SB Arts Media. 10–11 – zef art, Ysbrand Cosijn. 12–13 – Ollyy. 14–15 – Nadezhda Bolotina, Adrian Stanica. 16–17 – PeskyMonkey, Claudio Gabriel Gonda. 18–19 – Mark Winfrey, Dm_Cherry. 20–21 – Elenfantasia, Ekaterina Bondaretc. 22–23 – Vera Petruk, Glevalex, Goji. 24–25 – Oleg Golovnev, 3doorsofsun. 26–27 – Nastyaofly, Yevhenii Orlov. 28–29 – Albina Tiplyashina, Kiselev Andrey Valerevich. 30 – Denis Makarenko, Anatoliy Karlyuk.

# CONTENTS

WORDS THAT LOOK LIKE <u>THIS</u> ARE EXPLAINED IN THE GLOSSARY ON PAGE 31.

# THE ALIENS ARE COMING

How can we be the only ones in the universe? There are billions of planets in each <u>galaxy</u> and billions of galaxies in the universe! Earth can't be the only place supporting life.

Aliens must be real! There will be hundreds of alien <u>species</u> out there.

Would aliens come to Earth? They will know where to find us if they want to.

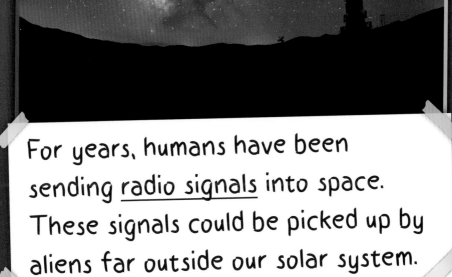

For years, humans have been sending <u>radio signals</u> into space. These signals could be picked up by aliens far outside our solar system.

# ALIENS OF THE PAST

It seems likely that aliens have already visited Earth before. We can see signs of aliens in old paintings.

Some of the earliest signs of aliens come from cave paintings. There are cave paintings over 10,000 years old that seem to show aliens.

Other things suggest the aliens did more than just visit humans in the past.

Many people believe the ancient Egyptians were visited by aliens. They think that aliens helped the Egyptians. That would explain why they were so <u>advanced</u> for their time.

# ALIENS OF THE PRESENT

There have been many recent things that suggest aliens have visited.

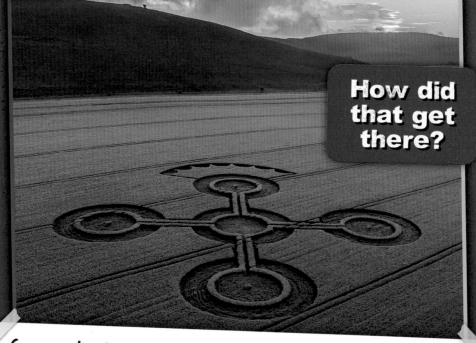

How did that get there?

Crop circles are huge patterns and shapes that appear in fields. They usually appear overnight. Some are made by humans, but others are left without an explanation.

There are also stories of people who have been <u>abducted</u> by aliens. Many of these stories have lots in common.

You see bright lights in the sky. Then, you are pulled up into an alien spaceship. You are returned to Earth a few days later.

# THE ATTACK

Aliens might have been helpful in the past. However, there are lots of aliens. Others might not be so friendly when they come to Earth.

Aliens could attack at any moment. You need to be prepared for when they do.

# METEORITES

One of the most obvious signs of an oncoming alien attack is meteorites. Scientists will insist that meteorites are just falling space rocks.

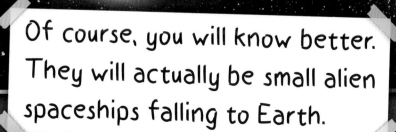

Of course, you will know better. They will actually be small alien spaceships falling to Earth.

# LIGHTS IN THE SKY

The lights you see in the sky might not be stars or even meteorites. Those could be the lights from distant alien spaceships.

Listen out for a strange humming coming from the sky. This could be a sign that the attack is about to start.

# ALIEN SPACESHIPS

The aliens may park their spaceships in our skies and wait. They might want to study Earth up close before they attack.

Other aliens might crash into the ground. Whatever the aliens do, you should head somewhere safe.

# PLACES TO AVOID

In the beginning, you won't know if the aliens come in peace. They might be here to take over Earth and <u>exterminate</u> all humans.

## BIG CITIES

Aliens will attack the biggest cities first. If you live in a big city, get away quickly.

TARGET ACQUIRED

# AREA 51

Area 51 is an American Air Force base in the United States. The US government does not share any information about what goes on there.

AREA 51 WARNING RESTRICTED AREA Use of deadly force authorized NO TRESPASSING

Many people suspect aliens are kept in Area 51. The attacking aliens might be rescuing their friends.

# HIDEOUT HUNTING

A good hideout will keep you safe during an alien attack. However, finding somewhere will be very difficult.

There are not many places on Earth that the aliens can't see. They might be able to scan an area for human life with their advanced technology.

You are going to need to be very sneaky to escape the aliens' technology. Getting yourself to a place where it cannot reach you is your only hope.

You might need to head to one of the most distant places on Earth.

An underground bunker is your best bet. You might not have to travel far if you know of one nearby.

Not everyone knows where to find a bunker. You won't have time to build one. You might have to travel to stay safe.

Go somewhere that aliens would not expect to find humans. This could be a desert, rainforest or place that is frozen, such as the Arctic and the Antarctic.

It will be tough hiding out in these places. Make sure you bring plenty of <u>supplies</u>.

# PEACEFUL ALIENS

Aliens might not have come to attack us. It is possible that they have come in peace.

The aliens must be pretty clever if they've made it all the way to Earth. However, they might not know some of the things that we do.

What could we teach aliens? Our brains are capable of understanding many things. We know lots about the universe, science and human emotions.

We could explain to them how life on Earth works. Who knows more about humans than humans?

Human <u>culture</u> could be interesting to aliens. Humans have lots to offer in terms of music, art and writing.

We sing and dance together. We keep animals in our homes as pets. That may be more important to aliens than science.

We have no idea what life is like for aliens. What is normal to us might be the most amazing thing in the universe to them.

Earth might seem like a great holiday planet for aliens.

# EVIL ALIENS

We are going to be in trouble if the aliens are not friendly. Alien technology is far more advanced than ours and could be deadly.

You need to work out why the aliens have come. Then, maybe you can stop them.

Aliens might be here to take Earth's natural resources. They could be after rocks, metals and gemstones.

Another resource is water. Earth has lots of water. The aliens might want to suck all of it up.

Aliens could get some of these resources anywhere. There are probably hundreds of planets with water and gemstones.

They might be after another resource. There must be something the aliens want that they can only get from Earth. They might want humans!

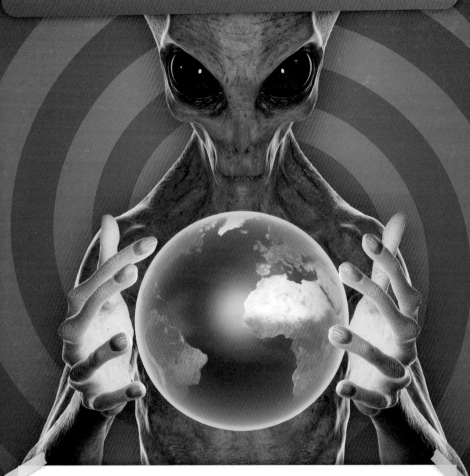

Humans could be a very useful resource to aliens. We have powerful brains. We have the ability to work together.

This would make humans great <u>slaves</u> for aliens. If they don't kill us all, they might take us back to their planet.

# LIVING IN THE ATTACK

Humanity will have to work together if it wants to survive.

There are nearly 8 billion people on planet Earth.

Each country has lots of weapons We would have enough guns and rockets to destroy lots of alien spaceships if we shared them.

It can be difficult to get everyone to work together. Humans have fought against each other for thousands of years.

An evil army invading Earth might bring humanity together. Earth is the one thing every human shares, after all.

# SURVIVING THE ATTACK

You might just survive the attack of the aliens if you hang on to this guide. It is important not to lose hope.

If any aliens set their sights on planet Earth, you'll be ready for them.

# GLOSSARY

**abducted** kidnapped or taken away by force

**advanced** beyond the basic level

**culture** the traditions, ideas and ways of life of a group of people

**exterminate** to destroy or kill a group of things completely

**galaxy** a large group of planets and stars

**natural resources** things that are not human-made

**radio signals** waves of light or sound that carry a message, sound or image

**slaves** people who are forced to work without pay and are owned by someone else

**species** a group of animals or plants that are similar and can produce young animals or plants

**supplies** things, such as food or equipment, that are needed for a particular job or reason

# INDEX